PRAYERS *and* BLESSINGS *for* YOUR HOME

ARTWORK BY

D. Morgan

HARVEST HOUSE PUBLISHERS

EUGENE, OREGON

O Lord, we come before Thy face;
In every home bestow Thy grace
On children, father, mother,
Relieve their wants, their burdens ease,
Let them together dwell in peace
And love to one another.

Magnus Landstad

PRAYERS AND BLESSINGS FOR YOUR HOME
Text Copyright © 2008 by Harvest House Publishers
Eugene, Oregon 97402
www.harvesthousepublishers.com

ISBN 13: 978-0-7369-2157-2
ISBN 10: 0-7369-2157-5

Artwork designs are reproduced under license from © 2008 Leo Licensing, LLC and may not be reproduced without permission.
For more information regarding art prints featured in this book, please contact:
    Leo Licensing, LLC
    8573 Medlin Road
    Baxter, TN 38544

Design and production by Koechel Peterson & Associates, Inc., Minneapolis, Minnesota

Unless otherwise indicated, Scripture quotations are taken from the Holy Bible, New International Version®, Copyright © 1973, 1978, 1984 by the International Bible Society. Used by permission of Zondervan Publishing House.

Verses marked RSV are taken from the Revised Standard Version of the Bible, Copyright © 1946, 1952, 1971 by the Division of Christian Education of the National Council of the Churches of Christ in the U.S.A. Used by permission.

Verses marked TLB are taken from *The Living Bible*, Copyright © 1971. Used by permission of Tyndale House Publishers, Inc., Wheaton, Illinois 60189. All rights reserved.

Harvest House Publishers has made every effort to trace the ownership of all poems and quotes. In the event of a question arising from the use of a poem or quote, we regret any error made and will be pleased to make the necessary correction in future editions of this book.

Printed in China

08 09 10 11 12 13 14 15 / LP / 10 9 8 7 6 5 4 3 2

Lottie

To

Dot

From

BLESS THIS HOUSE

HELEN TAYLOR

Bless this house, O Lord, we pray;
Make it safe by night and day.
Bless these walls so firm and stout,
Keeping want and trouble out.

Bless the roof and chimneys tall;
Let thy peace lie over all.
Bless this door, that it may prove
Ever open to joy and love.

Bless these windows shining bright,
Letting in God's heavenly light;
Bless the hearth, a-blazing there,
With smoke ascending like a prayer!

Bless the folk who dwell within,
Keep them pure and free from sin;
Bless us all that we may be
Fit, O Lord, to dwell with Thee.

Bless us all that one day we
May dwell, O Lord, with Thee!

As for me and my household,

we will serve the LORD.

JOSHUA 24:15

Crickets on a summer's night, a pilgrimage of birds in

Country gardens,
Gentle faces

Cozy little wayside places
These are things ...

6

flight

My Heart Embraces.

$\mathcal{D}$ear God, protect our going out and coming in; let us share the hospitality of this home with all who visit us, that those who enter here may know Your love and peace.

Author Unknown

The beautiful memories

We make in life

Will always
Be
Too
Few

But
The moments
That matter
Most
Of
All...

...Are
The
Moments
I spend
With
You.

8

O HAPPY HOME

O happy home, where Thou art
    loved the dearest,
Thou loving Friend and Savior
    of our race,
And where among the guests
    there never cometh
One who can hold such high
    and honored place!

O happy home, where two
    in heart united
In holy faith and blessed hope
    are one,
Whom death a little while
    alone divideth,
And cannot end the union
    here begun!

O happy home, whose little ones
    are given
Early to Thee, in humble faith
    and prayer,
To Thee, their Friend, Who from
    the heights of Heaven
Guides them, and guards with
    more than mother's care!

O happy home, where each one
    serves Thee, lowly,
Whatever his appointed work
    may be,
Till every common task seems
    great and holy,
When it is done, O Lord,
    as unto Thee!

O happy home, where Thou art
    not forgotten,
Where joy is overflowing,
    full and free,
O happy home, where every
    wounded spirit
Is brought, Physician, Comforter,
    to Thee—

Until at last, when earth's day's work
    is ended,
All meet Thee in the blessed home
    above,
From whence Thou camest, where
    Thou hast ascended,
Thy everlasting home of peace
    and love!

KARL J. SPITTA

So the short journey
came blithely to an end,
and in the twilight
she saw a group of
loving faces at the door
of a humble little house,
which was more beautiful
than any palace in her
eyes, for it was home.

Louisa May Alcott
AN OLD-FASHIONED GIRL

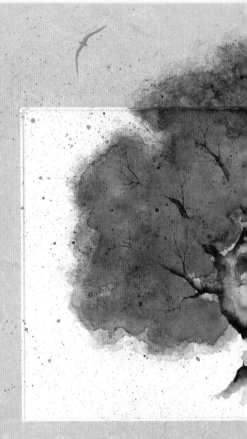

latch your door, may your troubles be less,

but happiness come through your front door.

Oh, to be home again, home again, home again!
Under the apple-boughs, down by the mill!

T.J. FIELDS

A house is built of logs and stones,
Of tiles and posts and piers,
A home is built of living deeds
That stand a thousand years.

Victor Hugo

Bless this land, Lord, that they who play, gather, and tend to it receive Your love and energy. Let this place be a place where neighbors, family, and friends gather to rejoice in life and to enjoy fellowship with one another.

AUTHOR UNKNOWN

A priceless pleasure
In life begins
When we discover
Good Neighbors...
...Good Friends

14

PRAYER TO ANOINT YOUR HOME

JEAN CHRISTEN

Heavenly Father,

Bless this house and the land that it sits upon.
Anoint both to be a holy place for our loved ones to gather.
Send Your heavenly hosts to descend upon it and station
them on the rooftop and in every corner, doorway, window,
and opening. May Your perfect love cast out all fear;
may Your perfect light cast out all darkness; and may
Your Holy Spirit fill the occupants of this home with love,
joy, peace, patience, kindness, goodness, faithfulness,
gentleness, and self-control.

May love and warmth greet and welcome each guest
the minute they walk through the front door. May this
house be a respite from the world for our family, friends,
and neighbors. May it sing with joy and laughter and glow
with peace and serenity. May it be a gathering place for good
people, and may it be a place where good things happen.

Amen.

I hear your footstep down the hall.
You are home again, and safe.

The burdens of the day are lightened
And all the night noises ...
... are Music

To My Ears.

$\mathcal{I}$ will make my people

and their homes around

my hill a blessing. And

there shall be showers,

showers of blessing,

for I will not shut off

the rains but send them

in their seasons.

Ezekiel 34:26 TLB

Happy the home when God is there,
　　And love fills every breast;
　　When one their wish, and one their prayer,
　　And one their heav'nly rest.

Happy the home where Jesus' Name
　　Is sweet to every ear;
　　Where children early speak His fame,
　　And parents hold Him dear.

Happy the home where prayer is heard,
　　And praise each day does rise;
　　Where parents love the sacred Word
　　And all its wisdom prize.

Lord, let us in our homes agree
　　This blessed peace to gain;
　　Unite our hearts in love to Thee,
　　And love to all will reign.

HENRY WARE

Bless this kitchen, LORD,
and those who gather here each day.
Let it be a place where we can meet
to love and laugh and pray. Amen.

Author Unknown

I wish you rainbows all around

Sit down and feed, and

*Laughter is
brightest where food is best.*
IRISH PROVERB

skies of blue above

flowers on your pathway

But most of all . . .
. . . I wish you love.

welcome to our table.
SHAKESPEARE

WHEN THERE'S LOVE AT HOME

JOHN H. McNAUGHTON

There is beauty all around,
When there's love at home;
There is joy in ev'ry sound,
When there's love at home.
Peace and plenty here abide,
Smiling sweet on ev'ry side;
Time doth softly, sweetly glide,
When there's love at home;
Love at home, love at home,
Time doth softly, sweetly glide,
When there's love at home.
In the cottage there is joy,
When there's love at home;
Hate and envy ne'er annoy,
When there's love at home.
Roses blossom 'neath our feet,
All the earth's a garden sweet,
Making life a bliss complete,
When there's love at home;
Love at home, love at home,
Making life a bliss complete,
When there's love at home.

Kindly Heaven smiles above,
When there's love at home;
All the earth is filled with love,
When there's love at home.
Sweeter sings the brooklet by,
Brighter beams the azure sky:
Oh, there's One Who smiles on high,
When there's love at home;
Love at home, love at home,
Oh, there's One Who smiles on high,
When there's love at home.

Jesus, show Thy mercy mine,
Then there's love at home;
Sweetly whisper I am Thine,
Then there's love at home.
Source of love, Thy cheering light
Far exceeds the sun so bright—
Can dispel the gloom of night;
Then there's love at home;
Love at home, love at home,
Can dispel the gloom of night;
Then there's love at home.

The sweetest

place I know

Home

We gather together to ask the Lord's blessing.

DUTCH HYMN

Bless this house,
  this sacred space,
Where beauty reigns,
  and soft refrains
Give refuge from the
  world we face.

ROBERT ALDRIDGE

Why do we love
  certain houses,
And why do they
  seem to love us?
It is the warmth
  of our individual
Hearts reflected in
  our surroundings.

T.H. Robsjohn-Gibbings

Whether skies are blue or grey
  We dream the night

24

Right
Into
Day

Far from worldly cares away
In our peaceful
...Mountain
Hideaway

'Tis sweet to hear the

watch dog's honest bark

Bay deep-mouthed welcome

as we draw near home;

'Tis sweet to know there

is an eye will mark

Our coming, and look

brighter when we come.

Lord Byron

The light that shines greets me like a friend.

Through the pines

Happy hours beckon — Home is...
...Just around the Bend.

best, or a pleasant mixture of them all.

J.R.R. TOLKIEN

Sit with me at the

homestead hearth,

And stretch the hands

of memory forth

To warm them at the

wood-fire's blaze.

John Greenleaf Whittier

The roses of springtime
Are with me
In my memory
All
Winter
long

Home is the sphere of harmony and peace,
The spot where angels find a resting place,
When, bearing blessings, they descend to earth.

MRS. HALE

Blue skies on my way

There's joy in the morning

My heart is filled with love...

...On this special day.

It is in the shelter of each other that the people live.

IRISH PROVERB

Bless this house, dear Lord,
   and grant us peace within.

Give us love for one another
   and most of all our friends.

Help us to love Thee, dear Lord,
   with all our hearts and souls

And we will never forget Thy
   blessing in this little household.

Glenda Evans

together